# BIRD

D0444754

## NEIL AND KAREN DAWE
### Illustrated by Joe Weissmann

A Somerville House Book

**WORKMAN PUBLISHING**
**NEW YORK**

*For all the children who have never seen the stoop of a peregrine or heard the booming of a bittern.*

*Thanks to Mr. Jim Dick, The Royal Ontario Museum, Toronto, and to Mr. R. Wayne Campbell, Royal British Columbia Museum.*

Workman Publishing
708 Broadway
New York, New York 10003

Printed in the United States of America

First printing October 1988

10  9  8  7  6  5  4  3  2  1

Copyright © 1988 by Somerville House Books Limited
Illustrations © 1988 by Joe Weissmann

Library of Congress Cataloging-in-Publication Data
Dawe, Neil.
    The bird book and the bird feeder.
    "A Somerville House book."
    Summary: An illustrated field guide to twenty-four backyard birds common throughout North America, from blue jays and juncos to sparrows and chickadees. Also discusses bird feeders, bird migration, nesting, and keeping a bird journal.
    1. Birds—North America—Juvenile literature. 2. Birds—North America—Identification—Juvenile literature. 3. Bird feeders—Juvenile literature. [1. Birds—Identification. 2. Bird watching. 3. Bird feeders] I. Dawe, Karen. II. Weissmann, Joe, ill. III. Title.
QL681.D38  1988
598.297    88-40225
ISBN 0-89480-614-9 (pbk.)

# Contents

Biologists call different kinds of birds species. But birds of one particular species may vary in color or size in various parts of the country: a Song Sparrow in Alaska doesn't look exactly the same as a Song Sparrow in New York. These different forms of the same species are known as races.

All the birds in this book are arranged in taxonomic order, which is how you'll find them in many bird books. Taxonomic order is a type of "family tree" that suggests how closely they are related to each other. So if you look up the chickadee, you know it's more closely related to the titmouse next to it than to the sparrows near the very end of the book.

# Birding Is Fun!

Birds offer an exciting world to explore. They're colorful, active, entertaining—and they are everywhere. Some amazing birds are even in your backyard! The Bird Book and Feeder will help you identify and get to know them and their fascinating behaviors. You'll learn what it really means to "eat like a bird," why birds take "dust baths," and how they "build fences."

All the birds in this field guide except for the dove and the woodpeckers are songbirds, or perching birds, and they can be seen at feeders across North America at some time of the year.

At the top of each species page there is a range map, which shows where the bird may be found. The colors indicate when a particular bird can be expected: blue in winter; yellow in summer; green all year round. The illustrations are not captioned male or female if the sexes are alike.

Watch the birds as they visit your feeder and you'll discover who prefers to eat at the table, who likes to picnic on the lawn—and what kinds of foods birds can't resist.

So set up your feeder, and while you wait for the first guests to arrive, thumb through these pages to find out who might be dropping by.

Good birding!

*American Goldfinch on a thistle.*

# What Is a Bird?

A bird is an animal. It has a backbone, is warm blooded, and walks on two legs, but so does a human being. It flies, but so do insects and bats. And it lays eggs, but so do salamanders, some snakes, and turtles.

What then makes birds different from all other animals? Only birds have feathers and a wishbone.

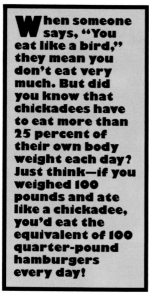

When someone says, "You eat like a bird," they mean you don't eat very much. But did you know that chickadees have to eat more than 25 percent of their own body weight each day? Just think—if you weighed 100 pounds and ate like a chickadee, you'd eat the equivalent of 100 quarter-pound hamburgers every day!

The bird shown here lived more than 140 million years ago. Scientists were excited when they found a fossil of this ancient creature. It looked a lot like a small dinosaur, but they knew it was a bird because it had feathers and a wishbone. And they knew they had discovered a very early bird because scales covered its head and it had teeth—something no bird has today.

Scientists named this early bird *Archaeopteryx,* which means "ancient wing," but it probably couldn't fly at all. Instead, they believe *Archaeopteryx* glided from tree to tree or ran along the ground scooping up insects with its wings.

In the millions of years since *Archaeopteryx* roamed the earth, birds have evolved into master fliers, partly by shedding weight—developing a lightweight bill and a gizzard (the strong muscle in their stomach that grinds up hard food) instead of heavy jaws and teeth, and hollow yet strong bones.

Today, many scientists think that birds are the closest living relatives of the dinosaurs. Imagine. Dinosaurs may not really be extinct after all—they may be visiting your feeder!

**D**id you know that a swan has more than 25,000 feathers, and that a tiny hummingbird has less than 1,000?

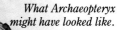

*What Archaeopteryx might have looked like.*

# A Bird's Anatomy

### third eyelid

A bird's eye has three eyelids. The upper or lower lid usually closes only when the bird sleeps. The third eyelid is a membrane that cleans and moistens the eye and protects it from drying out when the bird flies.

### gizzard

The grit that birds swallow lodges in the gizzard and helps grind hard food as the muscular gizzard contracts.

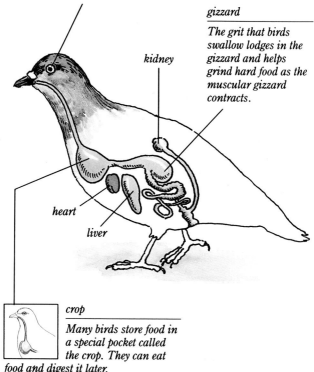

kidney

heart

liver

### crop

Many birds store food in a special pocket called the crop. They can eat food and digest it later.

*These three digits are all that's left of the bird's fingers since its arms and hands became wings. Because it has no hands, a bird uses its strong, light beak to gather food and nesting materials.*

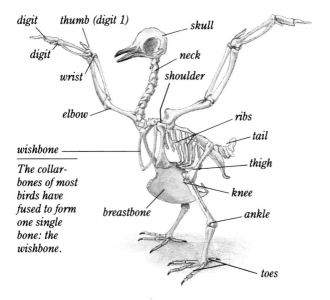

digit

thumb (digit 1)

digit

wrist

elbow

skull

neck

shoulder

ribs

tail

wishbone

*The collarbones of most birds have fused to form one single bone: the wishbone.*

thigh

knee

breastbone

ankle

toes

tendon

*All the songbirds that visit your feeder have tendons in the back of their legs that automatically lock their toes around a perch when they "sit." That's how birds can fall asleep on a branch without falling off!*

*Birds actually walk on just their toes. What looks like a backward knee is really the bird's ankle.*

9

# How to Identify a Bird

Birds usually are alert and move very quickly. Often you don't have time to get a long look at them. Here's what to look for when you want to identify a new bird at your feeder.

### Size
Compare the size of the newcomer to that of a familiar bird, such as a sparrow or robin. Is it larger or smaller?

### Shape
Is it plump or slender? Is the tail short or long, forked, notched, or squared? Does the bird have a crest on the top of its head? What shape is its bill?

### Color
If you have a well-lit view of the bird, color is the easiest clue to its identity. Don't just look at the color of the feathers, but also note the color of the bill, legs, and eyes.

### Habits
Does the bird climb down a tree trunk headfirst, or hang upside down at the tip of a branch? Does it feed on the ground or in the trees? Does it walk or hop?

### Flight
How does the bird fly as it comes to your feeder? Does it have a wavy flight path like that of a finch or a woodpecker, or does it fly in a straight line like a dove or a grackle?

### Voice
You can identify a bird without seeing it if you know its voice, for each species has its own unique song. A bird also has a call that can help you identify it. Some birds, such as chickadees, call their name.

# Field Marks

Field marks are those special characteristics that make each species of bird unique. Sometimes you can identify a bird by its color and shape; more often, you also need to look for breast markings, tail pattern, wing bars, rump patch, and eye stripes or eye rings. Once you've learned to "read" these field marks, you'll find it easier to identify the birds you see.

**Did you know a bird's bill is constantly growing and being worn down at the tip?**

crown
eye stripe (over eye)
lower bill
eye ring
upper bill
eye line (through eye)
nape
lore
wing bars
throat
rump
breast
tail
side
belly
outer tail feathers
whisker mark
(mustache)

*White-throated Sparrow*

# Setting Up Your Feeder

Whether you live in a city or in the country, in a house or an apartment, your feeder will attract birds. All you have to decide is whether to...

...hang it from a tree branch or your balcony;

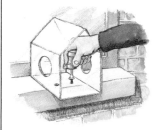

...screw it onto a post, windowsill, or platform;

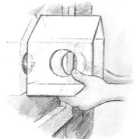

...or attach it to your windowpane.

Never use bare metal containers, mesh, or wire around your feeder. In cold weather, a bird's tongue or feet could freeze to the metal.

### Things to Check

- Is the ground around your feeder clear of shrubs?
- Can you see the feeder clearly from your house?
- Is your feeder reasonably sheltered from wind and rain?
- Will your feeder be easy to reach when there is lots of snow on the ground?

# BIRD FEEDER PROJECT

### Make a Landing or Feeding Shelf

If your window doesn't have a wide ledge, build a platform beneath it to encourage lots of birds to visit. Scatter seeds on the platform—and you've made a feeding shelf.

### Ground-feeding

Attract ground-feeding birds by scattering food on the ground. If you don't want seeds sprouting in your lawn, spread them out on a piece of plywood or use cracked grains.

### Pest Control

If cats or squirrels are going after the birds or their food, attach a large, square piece of wood on top of a post. Screw the feeder onto the center of the platform. Remember that some pests are great jumpers; place the feeder where it can't be reached from a fence, branch, or roof.

### Cleaning

Whenever you refill your feeder, make sure the seed tray is clean. If leftover seeds are water soaked or soiled by bird droppings, throw them away. Wash the tray in warm, soapy water; then rinse thoroughly. Wipe and dry the tray, and add a fresh supply of food.

13

# Food for the Birds

Some birds eat insects; others forage for seeds or fruits and berries; and some will eat a bit of everything. All birds need food high in protein and fat to fuel their bodies and provide energy for the many activities in a bird's life.

### Sunflower Seeds

Sunflower seeds are a favorite food of many birds and usually attract them like a magnet. Serve the seeds in the shell.

**DON'T put out bread or bread crumbs for the birds. They need a high-energy diet, and bread merely fills their stomachs while providing little nutrition. If a bird fills up with just bread on a cold winter's night, it may not live until morning.**

### Wild Bird Seed

Packages marked "Wild Bird Seed" contain a variety of whole seeds that attract many kinds of birds. If you want a less expensive food—or one that won't sprout on your lawn—buy Chick Scratch, a mixture of cracked grains. Add sunflower seeds for variety.

### Grit

Birds eat grit—small bits of gravel and sand—to help them grind up their food. No feeder should be without it. Oyster Shell is one type of grit carried by feed stores.

## Water

Birds need plenty of water for drinking and bathing. Make sure a fresh, clean supply is always available to them.

**If you feed birds in the fall, you MUST continue to do so right through to spring. Birds migrate to warmer places not because it's cold—but to find food. By putting out a feeder, you'll encourage some birds to stay in your area. Their lives depend on your feeder, so be sure to keep it filled all winter long.**

## Suet and Peanut Butter

Suet (hard beef fat) and all-natural peanut butter are good energy sources for birds in cold weather. Always mix flour or cornmeal with soft fats or peanut butter to absorb the grease; otherwise these foods might choke a bird, clog its nostrils, or rub off on its feathers—and greasy feathers won't keep a bird warm. Learn how to make a suet feeder on page 31.

## Special Treats

Whole or shelled peanuts and cracked nuts are popular; fruits such as berries, halved apples and oranges, and water-soaked raisins are other good choices; millet, hemp, corn, and thistle seeds are always welcome.

# Bird & Feeder Tips

THE BIRD BOOK will get you started as a "birder"— that's what enthusiastic bird watchers call themselves.

**1** Start keeping a record of the kinds of birds you observe, using the checklist on page 64. Some birders keep a "life list," which includes all the different birds they've ever seen.

**2** Your feeder is a new food supply in the neighborhood, and sometimes birds will take a while to find it. Don't be discouraged. Try setting out sunflower seeds in obvious places to attract their attention.

**3** Fast movements frighten birds, so move slowly and quietly when you're watching them.

**4** Listen for bird calls or songs to help you find birds that are out of sight. Try calling birds to you with a *psh-psh-psh-psh* sound.

**5** Take a close-up look at birds through 7 × 35 mm binoculars. If you wear glasses, use binoculars with rubber eyecups that can be folded back so you can place the eyepiece against your glasses.

**6** Birders keep a field notebook in which they record information about birds they've seen. Find out how to set up your own field notebook on page 26.

In summer, natural foods such as seeds, berries, and insects are so plentiful that fewer birds might use your feeder. The regulars, however, may bring their young to feed, and then you can have a close look at the whole family.

# Bird Behavior

Watch the birds at your feeder! You'll see that they have distinct personalities and their own special ways of reacting to each other, to other species, and to the environment.

Some behaviors are instinctive. When young birds leave the nest, for instance, they don't have to be taught how to fly—they just do it. Other behaviors are learned: the same young birds who just "knew" how to fly must learn to take off and land *into* the wind.

## INDIVIDUAL BEHAVIORS

When birds are alone, they act differently from the way they behave when they are with other birds or other animals. You might see a bird preening, bathing, sunning, yawning, stretching, or sleeping. You might see one scratching its head. Because birds cannot preen their head feathers with their bill, they use their feet. Some scratch their head by lifting a leg in front of the wing; others scratch with the leg over a lowered wing.

*A robin uses its foot to preen head feathers.*

## SOCIAL BEHAVIORS

When they're together, birds use their behaviors to "talk" to one another. Social behaviors include courtship and threat displays, songs and calls, and flocking. Displays are exaggerated movements or actions such as flashing bright colors, puffing out feathers, or strutting in front of an intruder. Each behavior has a meaning that other birds recognize and respond to in a set way.

**Did you know** that when most birds drink they dip their bill into the water, then tilt their head back to swallow? But some birds, such as pigeons, actually suck up the water much as you do when you use a straw.

*A male cardinal attacks his reflection, thinking it's another male in his territory.*

### Territorial and Threat Displays

Birds usually display rather than fight when there is a disagreement over food or territory (an area one bird has claimed as its own). Grackles move close together, their bills pointing high in the air; jays raise their crests; and finches lift their crown feathers and open their bills. The "winner" continues the display until the "loser" flees or turns away. Threat displays reduce the number of actual fights between birds, saving energy and preventing injury. During nesting season, some male birds attack their own reflection in a mirror or window to drive away what they think is another male in their territory.

**Did you know birds hear low-frequency sounds amazingly well? Some scientists think that birds can hear the sound of ocean waves crashing on a shore thousands of miles away! How helpful that would be to a migrating bird or a homing pigeon.**

### Calls and Songs

Birds also communicate through their calls and songs. Calls are used all year long to transmit information between mated pairs and among members of a flock, or to warn other birds of predators. Songs are used mainly by males during the breeding season to mark their territory and attract females.

Listen for two types of alarm calls. One warns of a predator on the ground or perched in a tree; this call is usually short, loud, and sharp. A soft call, longer and higher pitched, warns of a flying predator such as a hawk; this call, usually given from the protection of a tree or dense shrubbery, is a difficult sound for the predator to locate.

Birds may respond to these alarms by fleeing, mobbing the predator, or freezing (remaining motionless until the danger has passed).

### Peck Order

Within most flocks, each bird has a position and can peck, or "boss," only those birds lower than itself in the peck order. One bird, usually a male, is dominant over all the other birds. A peck order takes away the reasons for fighting because each bird knows its place in the flock.

## LOOK FOR

flocks of Mourning Doves visiting your feeder in the winter. When winter flocks break up and the birds begin to pair for nesting, it's a sure sign that spring is on the way. The mournful call of the males gives the bird its name. Their cooing is often mistaken for the hooting of an owl.

**FIELD MARKS:** This shy bird is larger than a robin. As it flies, watch for a long, tapered tail and white tips on the outer tail feathers. The Mourning Dove has a black spot on each side of the neck.

**FEEDER FOOD:** Mixed seeds, cracked corn.

**NATURAL FOOD:** Berries, grains, seeds, fruit, some insects.

**FIELD NOTES:** Both male and female Mourning Doves feed their young "pigeon's milk," a milk-like mixture that they make in their crop. When a nestling wants to be fed, it sticks its bill into the corner of a parent's mouth and the adult regurgitates, or pumps up, the pigeon's milk. Mourning Doves will feed on the ground and at your feeder.

21

## LOOK FOR

the way a woodpecker climbs, using its stiff tail feathers as a prop against the tree. Also watch how it flies—first flapping the wings and then gliding. All woodpeckers have an undulating flight pattern. In spring, listen for Downies "drumming" on telephone poles with their bill to attract a mate.

**FIELD MARKS:** This tame little woodpecker, slightly larger than a sparrow, has a short bill and a white back. Don't confuse it with the Hairy Woodpecker, which looks similar but is as big as a robin and has a long bill. Check for a red patch on the back of the males' heads.

**FEEDER FOOD:** Suet, fruit, cracked nuts.

**NATURAL FOOD:** Insects, insect larvae, spiders, berries, seeds.

**FIELD NOTES:** Unlike perching birds, which have three toes pointing forward and one toe pointing backward, woodpeckers have two toes forward and two back. This gives them a better grip on tree trunks when they look for food. Downy Woodpeckers drill into the dead wood of tree trunks in search of insects.

*male*

*female*

**FIELD MARKS:** The Northern Flicker, larger than a robin, is the only woodpecker you're likely to see on the ground. East of the Rocky Mountains the Yellow-shafted race is more common; west of the Rockies look for the Red-shafted race. A flicker with a mustache is probably a male.

**FEEDER FOOD:** Suet, peanut butter, fruit, seeds.

**NATURAL FOOD:** Insects, insect larvae, berries, seeds.

**FIELD NOTES:** The Yellow-shafted Flicker and the Red-shafted Flicker were once thought to be two separate species. But now they are considered different color forms, or races, of the same species that live in different places.

*Yellow-shafted Flicker male*

*Yellow-shafted in flight*

*Red-shafted in flight*

**LOOK FOR** the Northern Flicker's white rump patch when it flies. Bright markings that flash suddenly like this may startle an enemy, draw attention away from vital parts of the bird's body, warn other birds of danger, or help keep a flock together in flight.

## LOOK FOR

a Steller's Jay opening a peanut shell. Like the chickadee or titmouse with a sunflower seed, it holds the shell with a foot and pounds with its bill until the shell cracks.

**FIELD MARKS:** The raucous Steller's Jay is larger than a robin. This bird has a large black crest and light lines on its dark forehead.

**FEEDER FOOD:** Peanuts, sunflower seeds, suet, corn, cracked seeds.

**NATURAL FOOD:** Nuts, seeds, fruit, insects, spiders, frogs, snakes.

**FIELD NOTES:** The Steller's Jay is a loud, aggressive western jay. A noisy family group might come to your feeder, take over for a while, and then disappear. Watch as they glide in for a landing with their wing and tail feathers spread.

### BIRD PROJECT

Steller's Jays, Blue Jays, nuthatches, and titmice hide nuts in the ground, under leaves, on branches, or in cracks and crevices. In the autumn, set out unshelled peanuts around your feeder and watch where the jays hide them. The following spring, check to see if the birds have found them all.

**FIELD MARKS:** The noisy Blue Jay is larger than a robin. It has a black necklace, white markings on the wings and tail, and a showy crest.

**FEEDER FOOD:** Sunflower seeds, cracked nuts, cracked corn, peanuts, cut-up fruit.

**NATURAL FOOD:** Acorns and other nuts, seeds, insects, berries, and anything else it finds.

**FIELD NOTES:** The Blue Jay shrieks an alarm if a hawk or an owl comes near. Soon other jays join to "mob" the enemy, diving and screaming until they drive off the foe. If you get too close to a jay's nest, the parent birds might dive at you, too. At the feeder a Blue Jay will chase smaller birds away.

## BIRD PROJECT

Biologists have found that each Blue Jay has a unique black-and-white facial pattern. Sketch the facial markings of the jays that come to your feeder, and you'll find if the same birds are returning and how long they stay.

# Keep a Field Notebook

K eep a field notebook or journal to record all the birds that visit your feeder and what they do. Write down the date and your location at the

Black crown

Gray back

Dark eye

Black tail

Gray breast and belly

Rusty-red under tail

New bird at feeder. Saw it only for about 30 seconds with binoculars. Smaller than robin. Flew to feeder but was chased away by a jo Flew to bushes. Heard a like call a short while l Not seen again.

time, then list the birds you see. Count how many there are, and record how they act, their favorite foods, nesting activity, young, and when you first see them in spring and fall.

If you see a bird you can't identify, don't get your field guide—grab your notebook and a pencil instead. The bird you're looking at may fly off before you can identify it, so record its field marks, color, and behavior quickly. Note what other birds are with it and how they react to it. If you have time, sketch the bird. *Then* look it up in your field guide.

Your notes are a valuable record of the birds that use your feeder and visit your yard. And months later, it will be fun to read about the first hawk you ever saw or the first time a chickadee took food from your hand—almost as exciting as when it happened!

*Birders always carry a notebook.*

### BIRD PROJECT

**B**ecome part of Project FeederWatch. Bird watchers across North America send information about the birds at their feeders to Cornell University. The information is used to keep track of changes in bird populations and their winter ranges. If you want to participate, ask an adult who can verify that you know your birds to sponsor you and write to: Cornell Laboratory of Ornithology, 159 Sapsucker Woods Road, Ithaca, NY 14850.

**FIELD MARKS:** The chatty Black-capped Chickadee is smaller than a sparrow. It has a black cap and bib and white cheeks. In the east, the Carolina Chickadee is similar to the Black-capped but has paler sides, a smaller bib, and a shorter tail.

**FEEDER FOOD:** Sunflower seeds, suet.

**NATURAL FOOD:** Insects, insect eggs and larvae, spiders, seeds, small berries.

**FIELD NOTES:** Small, loose flocks of acrobatic chickadees hang upside down from branches and flit through trees and shrubs in constant search of food. At the feeder, the chickadee may take a seed, fly away to perch elsewhere and eat it, then come back for more. Listen for a *chick-a-dee-dee-dee* call or *fee-bee-bee* song.

### BIRD PROJECT

**A**fter chickadees are used to your feeder, stand very still nearby and hold a sunflower seed in your outstretched, open hand. Don't move, and a chickadee might take the seed.

**FIELD MARKS:** This eastern bird is smaller than a sparrow. It has a tufted gray crest and black forehead. A Black-crested race with a light forehead lives in Texas.

**FEEDER FOOD:** Suet, sunflower seeds.

**NATURAL FOOD:** Insects, insect eggs and larvae, spiders, berries, nuts, seeds.

**FIELD NOTES:** The Tufted Titmouse is a smart, inquisitive bird that often comes to the sound of people talking. It seems fearless and friendly, dropping down to take food from your hand or feeder or searching the branches above you for insects. The titmouse builds a nest from a variety of materials and has been seen plucking hair from a squirrel, a woodchuck —even a human.

*Red-breasted Nuthatch male*

*White-breasted Nuthatch male*

**FIELD MARKS:** The Red-breasted Nuthatch is smaller than a sparrow. It has a rusty breast and belly, a black eye line, and a white eye stripe. The White-breasted Nuthatch has a white breast and face. Females are paler than males.

**FEEDER FOOD:** Sunflower seeds, cracked nuts, suet.

**NATURAL FOOD:** Insects, insect eggs and larvae, spiders, seeds, nuts, berries.

**FIELD NOTES:** To crack open a nut, the nuthatch wedges it into the bark of a tree and then pecks, or "hacks," at the shell until the nut opens (that's why the nuthatch used to be called the "nut-hack").

---

**LOOK FOR** the way the nuthatch climbs headfirst down tree trunks. At this angle it may be able to spot food that is missed by other trunk feeders as they climb up the tree. Listen for the nuthatch's nasal-sounding *yank, yank, yank* call.

# BIRD FEEDER PROJECT

## Build a Suet Feeder

Suet is sold in supermarkets either in a solid chunk or ground up. Put a chunk of suet in a plastic mesh bag—the kind onions are sold in. Tie the bag so that the suet stays in place. Then hang it from a branch or tie it securely to the trunk of a tree.

Or find a log about 12 inches long and 4 inches thick. Ask an adult to drill some deep holes the size of a quarter in it. Let the suet soften at room temperature, then press it into the holes. Hang the log near your bird watching window. Or make a "mini-log" by pressing suet into a pine cone.

## Crunchy Suet Delight

Softened suet can be made into a super snack, bird style. Mix together equal amounts of suet, all-natural peanut butter, and mixed seeds. Then add enough cornmeal or whole-wheat flour (or both) to absorb the grease of the peanut butter.

Press the mixture into small plastic containers and refrigerate until solid. Unmold the treats and hang them in mesh bags.

# Feathers, Feathers, Feathers

Feathers are a bird's "clothes." They keep it warm, protect its body, and enable it to fly. The feather covering, or plumage, can be colorful like a male cardinal's or drab like a female House Sparrow's. In some species, adult males and females look alike. In others the female is a completely different color. Usually, the male has the most colorful plumage. In spring his bright colors attract a mate or warn other males away. The feathers of most females are less vivid, helping to camouflage them while nesting.

shaft

barbs

## Smooth Feathers

Smooth, firm contour feathers give a bird its shape and protect its body from heat and cold. The longest and stiffest of these are the flight feathers on the wings and tail.

Contour feathers have a center shaft that is hollow at the base. On each side of the shaft grow hundreds of rows of hooked barbs, which overlap and "zip" together to make a smooth, flat surface called the vane. Years ago people made quill pens from these feathers.

**LOOK FOR** feathers in your yard. If you find a feather with one vane wider than the other, you've found a flight feather from a bird's wing or tail. The vanes of contour feathers, which cover the body, are the same width on each side of the shaft.

## Fluffy Feathers

Soft, fluffy feathers known as down don't have any hooked barbs. They grow close to the bird's skin and keep it warm by trapping a layer of air next to its body. If you have a down-filled sleeping bag, you know how warm these fluffy feathers can be.

## Molting Feathers

All birds molt, or replace their feathers, at least once a year. Adult birds usually molt in summer, after the young leave the nest; some go through a partial molt just before breeding season as well.

*vane* —*shaft*

Songbirds lose their flight feathers in pairs, one from the same position on each wing, so they can fly while molting. Some birds, like ducks and geese, molt all their flight feathers at once. For a while they can't fly at all!

# Don't Robins Like My Feeder?

You've probably seen robins on your lawn tugging at worms, but why don't they visit your feeder? The answer is that robins seldom eat seeds. Try putting raisins and pieces of apple on your ground-feeding area, and your chances of attracting a robin will be better.

Like people, birds have their favorite foods and their favorite "restaurants." Some seed eaters, such as doves, prefer to feed on the ground below the feeder. Other birds, like starlings, forage for insects and insect larvae on the ground but will come to your seed feeder when snow covers the yard. And some, like woodpeckers, search for insects in the trees and shrubs. They may visit your feeding station only if you've included suet on the menu.

Tempt these birds during cold weather by putting out the feeder foods suggested on their species pages. You may be surprised at who drops into *your* restaurant!

*male*

**FIELD MARKS:** The American Robin is not the "little robin red breast" of stories—its breast is actually orange. This popular bird has a broken white eye ring, a yellow bill, and white-and-black stripes on the throat. The female is paler than the male.

**FEEDER FOOD:** Apples, raisins, cherries, grapes.

**NATURAL FOOD:** Worms, insects, insect larvae, berries, fruit.

**FIELD NOTES:** A robin swallows berries whole, one after another. Robins and other birds sometimes get drunk eating fermented fruit and berries, which can poison them if they eat too many.

**LOOK FOR** a robin cocking its head to one side, looking for worms. The robin has eyes on either side of the head and can see to the sides and front at the same time. But a sharp image is visible only through the center of the eye; to have a bird's-eye view of a worm, the robin must tilt its head and look through the center of just one eye.

## LOOK FOR

a mockingbird singing from a high perch in the fall. If you're keeping a record of how long a bird stays in your area before migrating, make sure it really is that bird you're hearing and not a mocker—who may continue to mimic another bird's song long after it has left the area.

**FIELD MARKS:** The robin-size mockingbird has yellow eyes and a long dark tail. It shows flashes of white on the wings and outer tail feathers during flight.

**FEEDER FOOD:** Suet, fruit, raisins.

**NATURAL FOOD:** Insects, spiders, snails, fruit, berries.

**FIELD NOTES:** The mockingbird feeds mainly on the ground but will come to special foods at feeders. This bird is not only a superb mimic of other birds' songs, but it has also been heard imitating frogs, dogs—even a piano! Both males and females sing in winter to defend their feeding territory.

*winter plumage*

**FIELD MARKS:** The European Starling is smaller than a robin. In fall and winter, the starling's black feathers are heavily speckled with white or tan and the bill is dark. In spring and summer, plumage becomes glossy black with a purple-green sheen and the bill turns yellow. The short tail helps distinguish it from blackbirds, cowbirds, and grackles.

**FEEDER FOOD:** Seeds, fruit.

**NATURAL FOOD:** Insects, insect larvae, worms, spiders, berries, seeds, grains.

**FIELD NOTES:** The starling, named for the little white "stars" on its fall plumage, gathers in large flocks during the day and in huge roosts at night. At the feeder, starlings are aggressive and can frighten other birds away.

**LOOK FOR** the starling's changing plumage through the seasons. This bird doesn't molt its speckled autumn feathers. Instead, the white feather tips wear off over the winter to reveal glossy black, springtime breeding plumage.

37

# Migration

Each spring and fall, more and different birds will likely be stopping by your backyard and feeder during their twice-a-year migration. Birds migrate to find new food sources and nesting or roosting sites.

In spring birds move from their winter home in the south to their summer nesting home in the north. There they find plenty to eat and can use the longer daylight hours to gather food for their hungry chicks.

In autumn, when the days shorten, birds and their young eat lots of food to add layers of body fat, a built-in energy supply for the long journey to their winter home. As the weather becomes colder, birds gather into flocks, until finally they start to move south. Along the way they stop, sometimes for several days, to find food and replenish their fat reserves.

Most songbirds migrate at night when they're safe from hawks and other predators. You may hear them calling to each other to keep the flock together. They rest and feed during the day, often at feeders. Some birds can travel hundreds of miles in one night.

Not all birds migrate long distances north and south. Some move from mountaintops to lowlands or from the interior of the country to the coast; others migrate each day from their roosting areas to feeding areas—perhaps your feeding station. Many don't migrate at all.

*Watching Canada Geese fly to their winter home.*

## BIRD PROJECT

**R**ecord in your field notebook the number and kinds of birds you see at your feeder. Note the date, too, and you will have a record of when migrants arrive and leave your area. Look for migrants next year around the same time.

*female*

*male*

**FIELD MARKS:** The cardinal is smaller than a robin. It has a pointed crest and a strong, cone-shaped bill. The male is one of the most brightly colored birds you'll attract to your feeder; the female is light brown.

## LOOK FOR

the different ways a cardinal holds its crest. Crested birds show when they're afraid, nervous, excited, resting, or about to attack by raising or lowering their crest. Other birds can read this "language."

**FEEDER FOOD:** Sunflower seeds, small seeds, raisins, apples, nuts, cracked corn.

**NATURAL FOOD:** Seeds, grains, berries, insects, insect larvae, fruit.

**FIELD NOTES:** This eastern bird nests early in the spring and then again, sometimes raising as many as four broods a year. The cardinal doesn't migrate, but young birds may travel long distances searching for new territory. Like many other finches, it has a thick, short bill that's perfect for cracking seeds.

a towhee kicking in leaf litter. Many birds stand on one foot and scratch the ground with the other, but the towhee scratches with both feet together. Birds that scratch this way are said to do so "towhee style." Listen for the sound of a towhee kicking dry leaves as it scratches for insects.

**FIELD MARKS:** The Rufous-sided Towhee is smaller than a robin. It has white tips on the outer feathers of its long tail; most races have red eyes. The western races have two white wing bars and white spots on the back. The western female looks like the male but is paler; the eastern female is brown above.

**FEEDER FOOD:** Mixed seeds, fruit, nuts, suet.

**NATURAL FOOD:** Insects, insect larvae, spiders, seeds, berries.

**FIELD NOTES:** The towhee is a loner, but in winter several may be seen at the same time around your feeder. All of its movements are quick. At the feeder or on the ground, the towhee flicks its tail constantly.

*eastern race female*

*eastern race male*

## LOOK FOR

the Song Sparrow flitting through the bushes, pumping its tail up and down. This may be the clue that confirms your identification. Listen for its melodious song, beginning with *sweet, sweet, sweet*. The female sings only before nesting season.

**FIELD MARKS:** The appropriately named Song Sparrow has a gray eye stripe, dark whisker marks, a heavily streaked breast, and a central breast spot. Eastern races are lighter in color than western races.

**FEEDER FOOD:** Mixed seeds.

**NATURAL FOOD:** Seeds, insects, insect larvae, berries.

**FIELD NOTES:** Song Sparrows are fast moving and shy. You will usually see only one or two at your feeder or on the ground below, and they will probably be the same birds each time. Your feeding station is a part of their territory and they'll be quick to defend it.

*eastern race*

# BIRD FEEDER PROJECT

More birds will come to your yard if you have a birdbath. A clean plastic dishpan with low sides and gravel in the bottom makes a good one. The bath should slope so the water is very shallow at one end and no deeper than the length of your longest finger at the other. Place it in the open away from shrubs, but close to the branches of a tree for protection from predators. Birds also like a nearby perch to preen on after they bathe.

To build a birdbath, dig a hole about the size of a garbage can lid. Slope the bottom, line the hole with heavy plastic, and add a layer of sand or gravel. Place a flat rock in the deep end, and slowly pour water on it as you fill the bath so you don't disturb the sand.

Birds are attracted to the sound of water dripping. Hang a plastic container with a very tiny hole in the bottom about two feet above the bath, and fill the container with water. Ideally, one or two drops of water should fall each second.

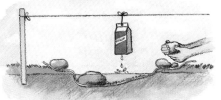

43

# Feather Care

Birds spend a lot of time preening, or taking care of their feathers with their bills. They do it for several reasons.

### To Zip Up Feathers

The hooked barbs on contour feathers sometimes come apart. As the bird pulls the feather through its bill, it is able to zip up all the hooks again.

### To Waterproof Feathers

Most birds have an oil gland at the base of the tail. By squeezing out oil with its bill and spreading it on the feathers as it preens, a bird waterproofs and conditions them.

### To Clean Feathers

When a bird preens, it gets rid of any dirt on its feathers and removes feather lice (tiny insects that can bite off parts of the bird's feathers and damage its

*Blue Jay taking a bath.*

plumage). Before preening, many birds take a bath—not to wash off dirt but to wet the feathers to make preening easier. First they dunk their head and breast underwater; then they raise their head high and flap their wings. Water sprays everywhere! After a bath, birds usually fly to a nearby perch to preen and oil their feathers, always starting with the important wing feathers.

*House Sparrow dusting its feathers.*

Birds take other kinds of baths, too…

### Dust Baths

When a bird flaps around in the dirt, it is taking a dust bath. By dusting its feathers and then shaking hard, the bird is able to get rid of feather lice. Look for a rounded depression in dry soil—that's a sign a bird has been dusting.

### Sun Baths

On sunny days you may see a bird lying on its side with its wing and tail feathers spread out—almost as if in a trance. Some biologists think a bird suns itself because it is then easier to find feather lice (which gather in darker places under the wings and tail). Others think a bird sunbathes because sunlight and feather oil together produce Vitamin D, which the bird swallows as it preens.

### Ant Baths

Ants release a strong acid that kills feather lice. In a behavior called anting, some birds crouch on an ant hill and let ants crawl all over them. Others rub crushed ants on their feathers.

*Northern Flicker anting.*

## LOOK FOR

a White-throated Sparrow eating a berry. The bird crushes the berry in its bill and then squeezes out the pulp by moving the bill back and forth. When finished, the sparrow drops the skin of the berry and starts again with another one.

*White-crowned Sparrow*

*White-throated Sparrow*

**FIELD MARKS:** The White-throated Sparrow has a white throat, dark bill, and yellow lores; some have tan stripes on their heads. The White-crowned Sparrow lacks the white throat and yellow lores and has a light-colored bill; immature White-crowns have rusty-colored head stripes.

**FEEDER FOOD:** Small seeds, cracked seeds.

**NATURAL FOOD:** Seeds, insects, insect larvae, plant buds, berries.

**FIELD NOTES:** White-throated Sparrows and White-crowned Sparrows prefer to find food on the ground but they will come to a feeder, especially in the early morning and late evening. In winter, these sparrows roost in small flocks in dense thickets and shrubs.

*Slate-colored Junco male*

*Oregon Junco male*

**FIELD MARKS:** The junco is a sparrow-size bird with white outer tail feathers. There are four different races of the Dark-eyed Junco, but the two most common at feeders are the Slate-colored Junco and the Oregon Junco. The females are lighter in color than the males.

**FEEDER FOOD:** Small seeds, cracked seeds.

**NATURAL FOOD:** Seeds, insects, some berries.

**FIELD NOTES:** The junco, often called "snowbird," travels in flocks that may regularly appear at your feeder. With much chasing and bickering, they forage on the ground for dropped seeds while a few of them take over the feeder. Juncos flash their tail feathers as they fly.

## LOOK FOR

one junco at the feeder that chases away other birds as it feeds. Birds have a pecking order within the flock—one male is usually "boss" and can chase away other birds of its kind.

# Roosting

We see birds all around us during the day, but what do birds do at night? Some birds hunt; others migrate in the spring and autumn; most of the time, most birds sleep. Their sleeping place is called a roost, and it must protect them from wind, rain, snow, and predators.

Woodpeckers may dig a hole in a tree just for roosting. Chickadees roost in old woodpecker holes or even in man-made nest boxes. Some birds sleep on the ground, and many roost in the branches of trees. Robins, cowbirds, starlings, and blackbirds often fly long distances to roost in mixed flocks of several million birds.

*Three chickadees tucked in for the night.*

Keeping warm at night is a big problem for small birds, especially in winter. They crouch on a perch and fluff their feathers to trap warm air underneath. Most songbirds sleep with their head turned and their bill tucked under the shoulder feathers. On really cold nights, many birds huddle together to conserve heat.

## LOOK FOR
the red shoulder patches of the male. In spring he displays by spreading his tail feathers, opening his wings, and flashing his shoulder patches. His display attracts females but warns other males to stay away.

**FIELD MARKS:** This blackbird is slightly smaller than a robin. The male is well named for his glossy black feathers and red patches on his wings. The female is brown with a heavily streaked breast and a light eye stripe. The Red-wing's bill is sharply pointed.

**FEEDER FOOD:** Mixed seeds.

**NATURAL FOOD:** Seeds, grains, insects, insect larvae, spiders, snails, berries, fruit.

**FIELD NOTES:** The Red-winged Blackbird is probably the most abundant land bird in North America. In winter it gathers in huge flocks, mainly in the south, often with cowbirds, grackles, and starlings. In spring it is one of the earliest birds to arrive in the north. Males arrive first and perch atop cattails in marshes, singing their *konk-a-ree* song. Unlike most songbirds, the male Red-winged Blackbird will allow several females within his territory.

*female*

*male*

49

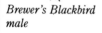

*Common Grackle male*

*Brewer's Blackbird male*

**LOOK FOR** the grackle eating nuts at your feeder. Hanging down like a knife from the roof of its mouth is a sharp plate. A grackle turns the nut against this plate until the shell splits, then eats the meat inside.

**FIELD MARKS:** The yellow-eyed Common Grackle is larger than a robin. Its head and breast have a purple sheen; some races have a bronze wash. The long tail widens at the end, and in flight the sides turn up into a V-shape. The coloring of the female is more drab than that of the male. The similar Brewer's Blackbird, more common in the west, is smaller than a robin; the female is gray-brown and dark eyed.

**FEEDER FOOD:** Mixed seeds, nuts.

**NATURAL FOOD:** Nearly anything, including garbage and worms.

**FIELD NOTES:** The grackle is a noisy, aggressive eastern bird; with head held high it seems to strut across the lawn. The Brewer's Blackbird looks like a mechanical bird, bobbing its head as it walks. Both will feed on the ground or at the feeder.

## LOOK FOR

the shape of the cowbird's bill. Compare it to the bill of the grosbeak (large and thick for cracking large seeds), the starling (long and pointed for probing lawns in search of insects), and the chickadee (small and short for picking insects out of tree bark). The shape and size of its bill is a good clue to what a bird eats.

**FIELD MARKS:** This slim bird is larger than a sparrow. The male is glossy black with a brown head; the female is brownish gray. The cowbird's dark bill is short and thick.

**FEEDER FOOD:** Mixed seeds.

**NATURAL FOOD:** Seeds, berries, insects.

**FIELD NOTES:** The Brown-headed Cowbird is parasitic—she lays her egg in another bird's nest and then flies away, leaving the foster parent to incubate the egg and raise the chick. The cowbird may lay as many as 12 eggs, each in a different nest. If you see a large youngster being fed by a much smaller bird, you've probably discovered a young cowbird and its foster parent.

*female*

*male*

51

_female_

_male_

**FIELD MARKS:** The male Purple Finch looks like a red—not purple—sparrow with a thick, heavy bill and a notch at the end of its tail. The female has a light eye stripe. Don't confuse the Purple Finch with the similar House Finch. The male House Finch has a brown cap and heavier barring on his sides, and the female lacks the eye stripe.

**FEEDER FOOD:** Sunflower seeds, mixed seeds, nuts.

**NATURAL FOOD:** Seeds, insects, fruit, berries, buds and flower petals of trees and shrubs.

**FIELD NOTES:** Small flocks of these birds might show up at your feeder one winter and not the next. Finches appear at feeders in years when their favored trees have few seeds. During courtship displays, male Purple Finches energetically sing and flutter their wings in front of females.

## LOOK FOR

a finch threatening a rival at the feeder. You may see the bird face the intruder, lean forward as if to attack, raise the feathers on top of its head, open its mouth, and perhaps flick its wings and tail. This is a threat display and is part of the language of birds. The intruder will usually lower its head and turn away.

# BIRD FEEDER PROJECT

Birds have favorite foods. Try this project to see which foods different birds like.

**1.** Gather as many of these foods as you can: sunflower seeds, pieces of apple and orange, raisins, suet, corn, millet, berries, peanuts.

**2.** Collect as many jar lids (all the same size and shape) as you have different foods. Place a different food in each lid.

**3.** Set the lids at least 6 inches apart on a board near the feeder, on a windowsill, or on the ground.

**4.** Observe and record the birds that come to your new feeding station. Keep track of what each bird selects. Is one food enjoyed by a lot of birds? As the weather grows colder, you may notice a change in what the birds choose—high-energy foods such as sunflower seeds and suet might be preferred.

Try dying one type of food, such as sunflower seeds or corn, with vegetable coloring. Place a different-colored food in each lid (the food should be exactly the same; only the colors should be different). Put out one tray with undyed seed, also. Which color attracts the most birds?

# Nesting

Nesting usually begins in spring when the male chooses an area for mating, nest building, and finding food. Then he stakes out his territory by singing. People build fences; birds sing songs.

The male sings not only to keep other males away, but also to attract a mate. Normally, most birds will not allow another bird—even one of the opposite sex—to come too close. If a pair of birds are going to get together to breed, they must overcome the urge to drive each other away.

*Grass-lined cup.*

Courtship displays are the solution. The male often shows off his bright feathers or puffs up his crest or breast plumage, flies above the female, or flaps, bows, and struts in front of her. He may even chase her. The Red-winged Blackbird flashes his striking red shoulder patches; the American Goldfinch flies high in circles, without its usual undulating flight style, singing all the while; the Song Sparrow sings exuberantly. If the female decides he'll make a good mate, she stays in the male's territory.

*Hanging nest.*

*Cross section of a tree trunk nest.*

During courtship some male birds, such as finches and chickadees, feed the females. In some species, such as doves and crows, males and females preen each other. These activities strengthen the pair's bond, reducing their instinct to fight and allowing them to work together to raise the young.

Choosing the nest location and building the nest can be a job for both birds or for only one, depending on the species. The nest might be a grass-lined mud cup on a branch, a hole in a tree with chips in the bottom, or an elaborately woven hanging nest. Birds use many materials to build nests: grasses, twigs, moss, mud, spider webs, feathers, and sometimes even their own saliva. Some birds don't use any materials at all, but instead lay their eggs in another bird's nest or in a simple scrape, or hollow, on the ground.

*Scrape.*

## BIRD PROJECT

In the spring, find out what nesting materials birds prefer to use by setting out finger-length pieces of string, dried grasses, twigs, hair, and feathers. Hang them over tree branches or in other places where birds will see them. Set out a container of mud, too.

# From Egg to Fledgling

When the nest is completed, the female lays her eggs—usually one a day—until the clutch, or total number of eggs, is laid. Most of the birds that visit your feeder lay from three to six eggs; doves lay just two.

For about the next two weeks, the eggs must be kept warm so the chicks inside can develop. Usually the female incubates them with the heat from her body, but sometimes the male sits on the eggs, too. In some species, the male does all the incubating.

*Mother robin incubating her eggs.*

When the chick is ready to hatch, it rubs its egg tooth—a small bump at the tip of the bill—against the inside of the shell. The chick has a strong hatching muscle in its neck to help it push the egg tooth up against the shell. Soon the young bird cracks the shell and pushes itself free of the egg. Chicks of some species are covered with downy feathers, and they can walk and feed themselves shortly after they hatch. But the birds that come to your feeder hatch chicks that are naked and helpless. Parents use their bodies to warm, or brood, the young until they grow feathers.

*A chick breaking out of the egg.*

## BIRD PROJECT

In late spring, wake up before sunrise to listen to the dawn chorus. Different birds sing at different times in the morning—some start when it's just getting light, but others wait till it's full daylight. See if you can recognize the songs of the birds, and note the times they start singing.

*Hungry young nestlings at breakfast.*

Parent birds are kept very busy over the next two weeks bringing food to their brood of nestlings. If you see a bird carrying worms or insects in its bill, it's probably taking food back to hungry chicks. When the parent arrives at the nest, the young birds gape, or open their mouths wide, and the parent stuffs food inside. The nestlings gain weight quickly and are soon fully feathered and ready to leave the nest.

Young birds seem to leave the nest when their instincts tell them the time is right. Sometimes the parents will encourage them by withholding food, by calling them, or occasionally by pulling them from the nest. Fledglings often leave before they can fly well. If you find one that can't fly properly, don't pick it up. Instead, watch quietly from a distance to see if the parents are still feeding it. They won't come to their young if you are nearby.

*Fledglings about to take wing.*

57

## LOOK FOR

the way a flock of Pine Siskins leaves the feeder. They fly in a compact formation, with all the birds turning one way and then another at the same time. No one knows how they do it. Listen for their wheezy, buzzy calls.

**FIELD MARKS:** Slightly smaller and slimmer than a sparrow, this tame bird is heavily streaked in browns with a yellowish wash over its wings, rump, and tail.

**FEEDER FOOD:** Small seeds, cracked nuts, suet.

**NATURAL FOOD:** Small seeds such as dandelion and thistle, seeds from cones, insects, insect larvae, spiders, tree buds.

**FIELD NOTES:** Many birds of the finch family, such as the Pine Siskin and the Evening Grosbeak, are attracted to salt. They can often be seen along roadsides, picking up salt that has been spread on the icy roads. Like chickadees and titmice, siskins will take food from your hand. Remember, though, never to move suddenly or you'll ruin any trust the birds have in you.

## LOOK FOR

the flap-and-glide, roller-coaster flight of a goldfinch. When rising, it flaps its wings and calls *per-chick-o-ree*. Then the goldfinch tucks the wings close to its body and plunges downward.

**FIELD MARKS:** Smaller than a sparrow, the male American Goldfinch looks like a bright yellow canary with a black cap, wings, and tail. The female is olive-colored, with darker wings and tail. In winter the male looks like the female.

**FEEDER FOOD:** Sunflower seeds, mixed seeds.

**NATURAL FOOD:** Seeds, especially thistle and dandelion, insects, insect larvae.

**FIELD NOTES:** In late summer, flocks of American Goldfinches, or "wild canaries," descend on thistle heads. You might think you see unusually large numbers of females feeding. That's because young goldfinches look like adult females.

*female*

*winter plumage male*

*summer plumage male*

*female*

*male*

**FIELD MARKS:** The Evening Grosbeak, a finch, is slightly smaller than a robin. It has white wing patches and a very large, pale bill that is strong enough to crush cherry pits with ease. In spring the male's bill turns a pale green.

**FEEDER FOOD:** Sunflower seeds, mixed seeds, nuts.

**NATURAL FOOD:** Seeds and buds of shrubs and trees, especially maple, berries, fruit, insects.

**FIELD NOTES:** If empty maple keys are raining down onto the ground, look up. A flock of grosbeaks might be at the top of the trees, picking the keys and nipping out the seeds. Evening Grosbeaks look like falling leaves as they flutter to the ground. They have a loud, distinctive call.

## LOOK FOR

large numbers of grosbeaks pushing and shoving at the feeder. If their favorite foods— seeds of maple and evergreen trees— are easy to find, they may not visit your feeder. But if the seed crops fail, large flocks move east and south looking for food.

60

# House Sparrow

**LOOK FOR** small flocks of House Sparrows at fast-food restaurants, waiting to clean up the crumbs. One reason for the House Sparrow's success in North America is that it is able to coexist with people.

**FIELD MARKS:** This common city bird has a thick, heavy bill. In winter plumage, the male has a smaller black bib, light bill, and tan crown. The female has a light eye line and streaked back.

**FEEDER FOOD:** Cracked corn, seeds.

**NATURAL FOOD:** Grains, seeds, insects.

**FIELD NOTES:** The House Sparrow, an Old World Sparrow, was introduced to North America in New York in 1850 and has since spread across the continent. The common pigeon, or Rock Dove, and the House Sparrow are the most common birds seen in our largest cities.

*female*

*male*

# A Place Called Home

Birds need a place where they can find food, water, and shelter and raise their young. That place is called their habitat.

Today, bird habitat is rapidly disappearing around the world. Birds that migrate south for the winter arrive at brown hillsides logged and cleared of trees where lush, green rain forests once grew. Often, wetlands are drained and filled for use by agriculture or industry. And as cities grow, they take over the wild places where birds used to live and find food.

You can do something to help by turning your backyard into an official miniature refuge and part of a series of backyard habitats across North America. Set up your feeder and keep it stocked with food. Build a birdbath so water is always available. Plant trees and shrubs that will feed birds in winter, shelter them in summer, and give them safe places to build nests and raise their young.

If your yard provides food, water, cover, and nesting areas on a regular basis, you can receive a certificate and registration number as a National Backyard Wildlife Habitat. Write to the National Wildlife Federation, 1400 16th St. N.W., Washington, DC 20036, for information on their Backyard Wildlife Habitat Program.

# Bird Index and Checklist

**K**eep a record of the birds you see by checking them off on this list.